HELL'S FLOWERS

Life's tough being a weed,
in a world obsessed with flowers,
when in fact no discrimination was made,
by either the sun or the showers.

HELL'S FLOWERS

Asmita Patwardhan

Highbrow Scribes Publications
New Delhi

HELL'S FLOWERS
Copyright © : Asmita Patwardhan

Published : 2023

Published by
Highbrow Scribes Publications
55-C, Jhang Appts., Sec.-13
Rohini, New Delhi - 110085
Mobile : +91-8826398333
            +91-7982333488
E-mail : highbrowscribes@gmail.com
Website : www.highbrowscribes.com

Typeset by: Shagun Graphics, Delhi-110086

Printed by Sai Blessings Press, New Delhi.

CONTRIBUTORS

Poet & Author: **Asmita Patwardhan**, Pune

Expert Inputs by:

Dr. Jyoti Shetty, MD, DPM Consultant Psychiatrist, Pune

Dr. Mridula Apte, Clinical Psychologist M.Phil., Ph.D.

Mrs. Preeti Kale Kashikar, Counsellor, internationally certified NLP Practitioner, Pune

Illustrations: **Tithee Dixit**, B. Arch, Pune

Cover credit: **Swaraj Kunchur**, Pune

Technical inputs: **Alaukika Shirole**, BA Psychology, Pune

Assistance for Book design and layout: **Anant United**, Pune

Special thanks: **Divija Bhasin**, MA, MSc Psychology, Mumbai,

Literary inputs: **Kavya Sharma**, Delhi

Literary Agent: **Lalitha Ravindran**

DISCLAIMER

All experts and professionals involved in the preparation, consulting, or advising the author, for this book, in any capacity are bound by and maintain professional confidentiality. No patient information was disclosed to the author at any instance. The mental health professionals referred in the book merely consulted the author and provided their personal advice. The book is neither a promotion for the individuals referred nor is anything said by the author or the mental health professionals in the book to serve as or supplement professional medical advice. In case of need, please see a mental health professional of your choice if you require medical advice. All names used by the author are fictitious and resemblance to any person, dead or alive is purely coincidental. The author does not have a professional degree in psychology and hence the contents of the book are purely for literary purposes. The author bears no responsibility for the medical accuracy of the contents of the book.

TRIGGER WARNING

All words on the contents page and certain words in the text of the book may trigger persons suffering from mental health issues. Please read at your own discretion.

DEDICATION

This book is dedicated to Swapna and Uttara,
Moms of special kids and inspirational women of strength!

THE RIDE

Our journey has been hardly linear,
most days can get perfectly insane.
We might exist in planes that are skewed
but so well aligned, our thoughts remain.

That, what your heart says, my mind overhears
I shelter you, from all your ghosts and fears.
We make it seem like a song and breeze
but we work harder than what appears.

We make bridges out of barriers
and break obstacles to make ladders,
Some days are calm, some are full of frenzy,
some days full of laughs, some painted sadder.

There were times, when we kept going in circles,
and reason spiralled completely out of control.
Both of us felt dizzy and disbalanced,
but we always had the other to hold.

We held onto our lives
like there was no tomorrow!
Taking it each day at a time,
whether it brought happiness or sorrow.

You brought colours into my life,
in big, bold and bright hues;
I'll be honest some of those shades,
Are not something one may choose.

You showed me the tones, the in-betweens
that I might have missed otherwise.
Black and white were the only extents
within which before you, I would analyse!

I am definitely a wider, deeper person
that without you I would have never been.
This journey I could do with no other,
you pointed to things I would have left unseen.

I always wonder if *you* want more!
What *your* dreams are, what do *you* see?
I'll ensure happiness is always by your door,
and promise that you can always count on me!

X

PROLOGUE

Some days are like sand paper.
By the end of the day your spirit
is scattered around like fine sawdust,
with buoyant parts floating around
in the inclined rays of the evening sun_
making ditch attempts to reach the stars.

Some days are like paint brushes.
They cover you from top to bottom
in a shade you are reluctant to carry.
The bristles leave marks upon your skin,
the undulating surface resists the coat.
Tiny bubbles rise, making feeble protests.

Some days are like conveyor belts.
They take you through the motions,
same sequence, same speed, just same.
Nothing about them elevates your senses.
A loop that plays over and over again;
making you want to jump, break free!

But, thank God, there are other days.
Days that are like paper planes:
easy, laidback, restful, calm, so silent _
They do not wish to compete or impress.
They just glide in with the wind and soar.

After all, only paper planes can teach you
that something that was written off
has untapped potential;
with the right thrust, it can reach new heights…

ACKNOWLEDGEMENTS

I would like to sincerely thank my family for their unwavering support. Especially my mother, my inspiration, my guide and my role model who introduced me to my saviour, "poetry".

BACKSTORY

"If my art inspires you to create more art, why not?" said Swaraj like a wise old man, but the truth was that he was only in his early twenties when we had this conversation two years back. Swaraj is a special young man, a talented artist, pianist and robotics enthusiast who is on the Autism spectrum, he has been very blessed to have a compassionate yet determined mother who keeps inspiring and motivating him to learn new things. Her goal is to make him as independent as possible; to help him discover and celebrate his various talents, passions and interests.

When she noticed that he has an inclination towards art, being an accomplished artist herself, she took him to the renowned painter Mr. Ravi Paranjape in Pune and under his tutelage Swaraj immersed in expressing himself through painting.

Swaraj's mother Swapna happened to show me a painting of a Datura plant that he had painted. Swapna has a green thumb and her garden had a myriad of flowering plants, yet Swaraj chose to paint a wild Datura, that he saw growing by a hillock. When she showed me the painting, something tugged inside my heart. She told me he said that he picked the Datura specifically because he felt bad that people were scared of its poisonous nature and steered clear of it. On a personal level, he was connecting with and perceived the angst of the flower for being side-lined and dismissed by humans. My mind couldn't begin to encompass the exclusion he and his parents must feel on several occasions because society is unsure and unaware of how to behave right around/with special children. The treatment meted out to them, ranges from extreme hurtfulness to apathy to indifference and each of these attitudes hurt in their own way, very deeply.

Omkar is on the Autism spectrum and this book is also dedicated to Uttara, who is his mother. I distinctly remember, when the pandemic hit and the lockdown was declared, her status on one of her social media accounts read, "Social distancing might be new to most of you, but for people on the Autism spectrum and their parents and caregivers it is something very very (*sic) familiar. Not being able to interact with people in groups or at parties, being homebound for months, not welcomed in most social gatherings, or just making a brief appearance, unable to go to crowded places, no movies, no plays ...been there done that for years"!

Something broke inside me when I read that status and it spoke the same language that Swaraj's Datura did. The painting embodied, a sense of exclusion to the hilt. Hurt was portrayed so poignantly in that bright green picture staring back at me that before I even realised, I had written "Devils trumpet." This poem, which happens to be a part of this collection was inspired by Swaraj's art and the lives of his family, and him and many others who feel excluded and side-lined. I wanted to share the poem on my social media along with his artwork and hence reached out to his mother to seek his permission. He first read my poem and said that he wanted to speak to me personally.

I met him one morning and we spoke about standpoints and perspectives, about perceptions and prejudices and he was really befuddled about two things; one, that I understood what was being said between the lines in his painting and second, that it moved me so much that I felt the need to create more art. We connected then and there, as human beings and that conversation we had, gave me an insight into his sensitive, pure soul.

"Can I please share your beautiful painting with my poem, Swaraj, I asked?"

"If my art inspires you to create more art, why not?" said Swaraj.

His quiet agreement, the respect he gave to my work and the way he recognised my genuine intent, left me incredibly humbled and awestruck, to see that his complex mind could process my intention with so much clarity and insight.

Through the course of the last decade or so, mental health warriors have had a special place in my heart. This includes people with mental health issues, their caregivers, therapists and doctors who relentlessly fight each day with mental health issues.

Poetry was the medium that helped me heal from my own issues and hence a series of poems were written by me that centred around the theme of mental health, to create awareness and to give a word form to the struggle. Inspired by the lives of these brave children, women and men who battle the unseen and unknown enemy each day, every poem in this collection is about a certain person or an event or experience which is very personal to me.

Red spider lilies are called Hell Flower in Japanese Culture hence Swaraj's white lilies gave me the idea of titling the book as Hell's Flowers. It resonated with me very deeply because I feel that people who are dealing with mental health issues are trapped in their own hell. Also, we are the 'chosen ones,' God intended to make us in a certain way and that the factors around us, either made us or broke us.

This book has three sections, referred to as Gardens. These are not well-groomed, well-maintained, manicured gardens, but these are wild, overgrown, complex environments that become our private penitentiaries. Children are secretive, adults hide behind façades and the elderly are lost into a hazy realm. Hence this book is organised as Secret Garden, Hidden Garden and Forbidden Garden to focus on issues of different age groups.

In order to cope with depression due to chronic illness, I began writing poetry. The poems in this collection on one hand identify and understand the pain behind dealing with mental health issues, but on the other hand, their intention is to propel and motivate people to seek help and find their way out of these dark gardens, take a step towards daylight and take a whiff of fresh air.

CONTENTS

SECRET GARDEN

Birth - 20 Age group

THERAPIST THINKS

Dr Mridula Apte

Pune, Clinical Psychologist M. Phil, PhD

When we counsel children in the clinic, we generally try to understand the child holistically. We try to get as many inputs as possible about the child. Formal assessments are done when needed. Then, a treatment or therapy plan is made and suitable referrals to other professionals are appropriately made. Often children need a team approach, so more than one professional could be involved. Along with the therapy of the child, parental psycho-education and regular hand holding are important. Parents often tend to blame themselves for their child's issues. It is important to treat parents as an ally in the treatment of the child instead. Children normally respond beautifully to all kinds of evidence-based therapies and interventions.

INVISIBLE TAPE

Focus: breaking point

I will not break, as I'm held together
with an invisible tape.

I could have fallen apart but an unseen stitch
holds together, pieces of my broken heart.
My shoulders ache, with the load they take.
Too much at times, for their own sake.
My gut feels hit, where anxiety kicked,
and remorse bit.

My throat is clasped holding back sobs,
while surrendering to heavy gasps.
My feet are sore, their soles are worn,
from all the journeys they've borne;

Yet my spirit breaks out into an uplifting song,
for life is known, to relent and give in,
When you decide to keep going on and on.

DEVIL'S TRUMPET

Focus: Autism spectrum

I'm the proverbial Devil's trumpet-
Nature chose to taint my stream,
although I'm quite friendly
to you, I'm off the beam.

You'd rather be with red roses,
enchanted by their heady fragrance.
Or walk amidst the orchids,
soaking in their haughty arrogance.

Roses mind you, bear thorns;
go near one and be pricked for sure.
Orchids may be pretty flowers
but they are just a two-day wonder.

Come sit by me for a while,
give me a chance to bare my soul!
You'll discover something completely new
that with our inconsistencies we are whole.

STRANDED

Focus: PTSD

Do you often visit the place you were hurt?
Have you turned it into a twisted shrine?
Does every visit renew the anguish?
Does it ache, each time you look behind?
Does every trip down memory lane,
make you more vulnerable and insecure?
Do you keep making plans to go elsewhere
but are led back by a dubious detour?
Does navigating the roadmap of life,
keep making you cruise in circles?
And the only landmarks that keep surfacing,
Are red flags and vicious whirlpools that gurgle?
Does quicksand keep you trapped in one place?
Or a prison confines you to an open cage?
Sometimes souls get stranded someplace
and life seems nothing short of a wreckage.
The only treasure on this deserted island
is your beautiful irreplaceable soul;
Take it with you and fight the waves~
you'll find resolve as you stitch yourself back whole.

MIND THE COMPANY

Focus: negative thoughts

Imagine, that for a day you are left
with just your mind for company,
Will it be your darkest nightmare?
Or an orchestra playing a symphony?
Will it be an arduous ordeal
you desperately want to end!
Or will it be a fantastic adventure
filled with twists and turns and bends?
Will it be hours of total silence
spent in quiet retrospection?
Or will it be filled with cacophony
like a gridlocked intersection?
Slay the demons, shape your thoughts_
Clear the residual negativity,

So, when you are left alone in its presence,
Your mind is filled with peace and serenity!

FATE

Focus: difficult circumstance,

I've simply resolved with my fate not resigned to it!

MIRROR IMAGES

Focus: body image issues

The moon has been sending me messages
of wisdom with a hint of pathos.
This shape shifter, is all along
spelling out signs sent by the cosmos.
No matter what shape you are in
you might wax and wane in vain.
Don't ever hide your radiance,
Shine on don't ever refrain!
Our bodies may be transformed,
they might be a tad bit deformed.
What is important is not the outer shell
but that the spirit remains unharmed.
There are nights as dark as doom,
when the moon is totally shrouded.
Wait - give it just a little time,
A crescent will emerge, don't doubt it!
Make sure you hold onto your inner glow,
each night your strength will be tested.
Breathe, smile and accept yourself,
Your shining light will not be wasted.

PERFECT OFFERING

Focus: inner dialogue

(Inspiration for the poem: Opening lines by Leonard Cohen)
"Ring the bells that still can ring,
Forget your perfect offering"
Forget the things that hold you down,
Green leaves are unafraid of brown.
With every attempt you are conquering,
"Forget your perfect offering!"
Forget things that make you hesitate
Grey goslings, learn to levitate.
With self-belief as the wind under their wing,
Trying your best is the perfect offering!
Forget the things that discourage
Most certainly the world is not a stage,
There is no audience, so stop performing,
"Forget your perfect offering!"
All you need is to wake and rise each day
Shovel the stench of doubt from yesterday.
Take charge of life, don't let go off the steering,
"Forget the perfect offering!"
Someday you'll realise, what matters in the end,
Is that you navigated every twist, turn and bend_
Finally, journeys are all about experiencing,
So, forget your perfect offering
Ring the bells that still can ring
Your tiniest, steady progress is your perfect offering!

BROKEN BUT NOT BEATEN

Focus: bullying

Each time you would break me
I would disintegrate into fine dust.
So fine, that the gentlest breeze
felt like a gust of wind
that scattered parts of my being
to the farthest end of the horizon.

Each time you would break me,
I would walk for miles and miles:
Barefoot, across barren, sunburnt lands
searching and rummaging
to get back every bit
that you callously flung away.
As if no part of me was consequential.

Each time you try to break me now,
the choice will be mine, all mine.
Whether I simply continue to exist
as thousand broken pieces,
Or I search and heal and seal,
every broken bit of myself
to be whole again.

Next time you try to break me,
I will resist, with all my might.
For I have managed to keep
my hurt but scathed, identity alive.
It will help cement every crack,
filling the voids with courage.

No one can break me now_
For the broken seldom live in fear,
their strength lies in their fragility!
As they've realised the ultimate truth_
Stop questioning why and how you broke,
convince yourself, there are ways to mend and fix it.

ON US

Focus: baby steps

I saw the word 'onus' today being flung around callously,
it broke down and split into 'on us' like an eerie epiphany-
Praying for miracles without doing one's bit is definitely a fallacy.

BE AFRAID

Focus: self-harm

Be very afraid for the ones who are smiling,
Slightly wider smiles, slightly unnecessary smiles.
Be really petrified, for the ones at the top of their game.
Go past the modesty, or the haughtiness
Be really worried for the unattached,
Dig deeper and question, the frivolity and disregard.
Be really scared for the fiercely independent,
Break down their walls, find out what's seething inside_
Definitely worry about the ones seeking help,
A little less maybe, for they are a little ahead in this journey.
But do not leave the others to their own devices,
Talk, look in the eye, observe
and open channels of communication,
Silent screamers are the ones that need the most urgent help,
Sometimes we need to extend help
way before they know they need it,
If you can spare a few moments listening to the unsaid
and hearing the unspoken, you might be able to prevent,
the unimaginable and avert the unfortunate.

SLEEP SNATCHERS

Focus: ills of social media

I opened the mailbox yesterday, there was a strange invite,
I was summoned for a luncheon, which was
scheduled at midnight.
Curiosity got the best of me, I dressed up for the occasion,
The dress code was rather cryptic, it said,
Create your own illusion!
Punctuality is not my middle name
but I was so intrigued by this mystery,
When I pulled into the driveway it was exactly eleven fifty-three;
I parked my modest little car amongst a herd of metal beasts,
I should have picked up clues then,
instead of just handing over my keys

The grand dining room was almost full,
with just one seat remaining free,
I was escorted to the empty chair by an elderly Maître D,
All around me were these people
throwing about an air of aristocracy,
I felt really out of place as I've got a master's in inadequacy.
The person at the head of the table raised the finest crystal glass,
"Vampires of the twenty-first century", he said,
"Welcome to your first class"!
An icy chill went straight down my spine,
my eyes darted towards the door,

There was nothing but a solid wall,
from where I had entered before.
No one but me was horrified; they all held a haughty demeanour,
While I was sure everyone could hear the beating of my heart,
Oh! The crazy clamour,
I quickly rose to put in my protest,
my voice cracked as I said, "Excuse me,
I think there has been a terrible mistake,
I'm no vampire it's just plain, ordinary me!"
The chairman of the vampires quizzically raised a thick eyebrow,
Looking above his monocle he looked at me
as if I was a mad old cow,
"Oh, but you are our student of the year,
you were nominated by the jury,
With vampire skills as superior as yours,
you must be aware of that most surely."

I was aghast by this point this was the most
absurd thing I had heard.
What was going on around me,
was completely nutty and obscured.
"Wait a minute," I said "I get it! This is just one big prank,
Where are your capes, your red eyes?
Where have you all hidden your fangs?"
The entire table burst out laughing,
a low gut-wrenching kind of guffaw,
"Oh, we are no blood sucker's silly woman,
we don't go about flaunting claws,

We suck time, peace and space,
we are the proverbial digital intruders,
Sucking at your resources every day,
we are now the invincible marauders."
"I don't understand why I am here?
I'm not a vampire of any kind,
Please allow me to go away, I'm going right out of my mind!"
"Oh, but you are a vampire, the best that you can find,
you suck on emotions and feelings,
leaving pages and pages of poetry behind,"
"Your victims are poor hapless people,
that get so influenced by your words,
they jump onto any digital space,
where their emotions are easily stirred."
"That's when and where we find our prey,
our victims enter the virtual web,
We rob them of their sleep and rest,
altering their lifestyles and mindsets.

"No!" I shouted loudly, as I sat up in my bed,
I had been dreaming all along,
but is this what I subconsciously dread?

BEST VERSION OF YOU

Focus: being yourself

Don't do anything by half measures,
Weep, till your heart bleeds out all tears,
Scream, till your turmoil turns hoarse,
Love, with abandon, unabashedly, unconditionally,
Worry, justifiably and wear your wrinkles like trophies,
Hope, till the last vestiges of doubt vanquish,
Speak, frankly, unafraid to mirror your mind,
Share your wounds and triumphs with equal candour,
Accept your failings but also forgive yourself,
Live up to the challenge of playing the lead role in your life,
Write your own destiny leaving behind love, as your only legacy,
Treat everyone with the same empathy you seek for yourself,
Judge no one because bias clouds prudence,
Pray earnestly that ignorance is defeated by reason.
Rise after every fall with vengeance, as well as humility,
There's just one you, so make it your best version.

THE ENEMY WITHIN

Focus: inner dialogue

We tell children so many things
"Don't go out alone! You may get lost or taken,"
What about,
"Don't go into the back alleys of your mind,
it's a dark sinister place"?
"Don't talk to strangers! They can mislead you."
What about,
"Don't listen to your mind! It can make you lose your way."
"Look on both sides before you cross.
Or you will be accidentally hit."
What about,
"Don't enter one-ways in the mind!
They are vortices waiting to suck you in,"
"Knock on doors before entering.
It's rude to just barge in."
What about...
"Never open certain doors in the mind.
They are traps in disguise."
"Don't take candy from anyone.
It could put you in a dangerous situation,"
What about,
"The mind can play incredible tricks on you"?
You are unable to separate illusion from reality!
While we are warned about
every single danger that exists outside,
How easily the enemy within is forgotten!

HIDE

Focus: wrongdoing

The skin is called the hide for a reason
it skilfully shrouds the scars of the soul
to acquiesce wrong doing is an act of treason
when you offer a safe sanctum to a troll.

MORTALS

Focus: making mistakes

Don't go walking in my shoes,
Now, don't you get me wrong!
It is not about ownership,
or that to me they do belong.
It's just that I know how to wear
this weather-beaten sole,
only I know where the stitch cuts
and where there is a gaping hole.
I'm aware that my foot wobbles,
when I place it at a certain angle;
Or just how to pace my steps rightly,
to avoid painful kinks hurting my ankle.
Wear your own shoes, my child
Wear them with utmost pride
No matter how tattered they are
don't try to cover, trade or hide
They are solely yours and yours alone.
People might scathingly scoff or judge,
trust me they are perfectly built to bear,
stones, sticks, slurs and the sludge.
Walk with your head held high
even if your feet happen to falter_
Keep correcting your stride as you move along,
For we make mistakes, we are mortals!

THE CROW SONG

Focus: judgement

So easily we write off the
omnipresent cawing crow,
not giving him the slightest chance
shooing him off from every window,
cursing his incessant squawking,
openly showing displeasure
upon his ominous perching.
All we want is complete erasure,
assuming that he's spewing,
cantankerous-- crude curses,
thinking that all he is disgorging are
acerbic verbal abuses;
Maybe he's actually, in fact
circumventing claptrap cogently.
Maybe to him, he's singing
a crow song mellifluously!
Maybe his only fault is that
he's simply tone-deaf and can't hear himself.
What does it say about the rest of us?
Who writes off others only on prejudices ?
Appreciating a crow's song
is truly an acquired taste,
you can only discover its worth,
If you are open-minded and preconceptions can be erased.

WING SPAN

Focus: lack of self-belief

All along I kept waiting for rigid doors to cut me slack,
while they wrote me off as insignificant.
Do you know what was holding me back?
The width of my own wingspan,
was overwhelming and scared me;
So, I just chose to keep my wings folded,
because of this unrelenting insecurity.
Do we really acknowledge our gifts?
Are we brave enough to own them with pride?
Can we say to the world, "Look, I have arrived!"
And from arc lights that shine, do we not hide?
I waited for the doors to open, I kept thinking of lost
opportunities,
But when I learnt to stand up to my full height,
Doors burst open and I stepped out free…
Finally, what lay beyond was a land of contentment,
Only one golden rule was followed there, which was sacrosanct,
if you are real and won't shy away from being yourself,
your citizenship was deemed to be permanent.
Sometimes it is our own light that blinds us;
Our wingspans are wider than most doors.
Take just one step and cross that threshold,
nothing will stop your flight anymore.

NO SUPERPOWER

Focus: feeling insignificant

I always wonder, how so many people say
that if they could have one superpower
they would want the power of invisibility.
I don't think they have any idea
how powerless being invisible is?
The disrespect that comes with being looked through,
The rejection that comes with being disregarded,
The knowledge that your physical presence
is as unnecessary as your soul's existence.
The overwhelming sadness that comes,
with the idea of being hollow:
The disbelief that comes with seeing
that someone's eyes do not seek you out.
The sense of abandonment that comes
with being denied acknowledgement,
No, there is no power in invisibility…
For a planet that is so overly populated
it is invisibility that is taking up the most space.

PURSUIT

Focus: need for perfection

Why do we keep searching for....
The perfect time, the perfect reason,
The perfect day, the perfect season,
Why do we keep searching for...
Someone's approval, someone's intent,
Someone's motives, someone's consent,
Why do we keep searching for...
The right opportunity, the right time,
The right feeling, the right kind of sign,
Why do we keep searching for...
Something perfect, something divine
Something romantic, something sublime,
Why do we keep searching for...
Unrealistic goals, unrealistic visions,
Unrealistic outcomes, unrealistic transitions
Why do we keep searching at all?
If there's more then go seize it, seek it!
If this is all, make the most of it, work it!
Tomorrow can wait let's embrace the now
In the knowledge that the gift of life
will make everything right somehow,
Life's a game that unfolds backward
Crawl, run or sprint inching forwards,
Let's be our own official cheerleaders

Le's be the platoon as well it's leader
We are finally only human ....
No mystery, enigma, or the one seeking fame,
we all are finally just human...
Not contestants, players or rats in a race
The pursuit of perfection is futile
let's just choose our own pace
The pursuit of perfection ends here
for after all, it is an unreasonable game !!

WORK IN PROGRESS

Focus: inadequacy

When you feel alone and hurt_ I am always here.
I feel every wound, every pain, every fear,
when you are lost, you will find my hand.
Won't let you stray; I'll show the way.
If you fall and feel you cannot rise
I'll dust, but you pick yourself up, never give up.
If at some point you feel everything is pointless,
let your attitude remind you of gratitude.
If you feel unloved and friendless, for its cold out there,
I'm your sounding board, I care.
If you feel the world simply doesn't get you right,
walk your stride, let your heart feel light.
Some of our rough edges we can never smoothen,
keep preening, your plumage is beautiful and bright.
We are all works in progress and that is the only insight;
but most importantly if you ever feel unworthy
and times are particularly tough,
remember, to me you will always be enough.

FALLEN WINGS

Focus: losing hope

We are like rain termites
that frantically fly,
putting up feisty fights
screaming soundless sighs,
Dying every second
living for a flash,
floors full of fallen wings,
and hopes destined to dash!
But if your life span is a day
live it to the fullest
soak in the warmth of love
for that tiny portion, that came your way
was genuine and the purest.

DON'T LOOK BACK

Focus: bullying

Don't look back, whatever you do,
just don't look back.
Have faith, take that unfamiliar path,
The flames will ebb off of this aftermath,
Escape now, this is your chance to flee.
Behind you there is destruction, debris,

Broken spirits, broken hearts,
empty promises, torn apart,
Ugly voices, unkind words,
Slurs and allegations painfully spurred,
But you rose above it, standing tall
You did not let your fortress fall
Picked up all the shattered bits,
You were never the one to call it quits.

Don't look back,
whatever you do, don't look back…

You are building back your life again,
the road ahead may seem a circuitous route,
Change has swivelled the direction of the wind vane,
Life, may be obscured by the mist of doubt;
Just carry the lessons that you have learned.

Keep guarded safely the respect you've earned,
The future may seem hazy and blurred.
Soon, the clouds of uncertainty will be cleared_

You are not a victim but a warrior instead,
Don't saunter about, resolutely surge ahead,
Reclaim your life, live it to its full measure
Clear your slate with complete erasure,
Don't look back, whatever you do, just don't look back...
Your future holds a promise of a stunning comeback!

GODDESS

Focus: right upbringing

Raise her so that she knows
she is your pride and joy,
she's Shailaputri.

Raise her so she believes
that she can attain all her goals,
she's Bramhacharini.

Raise her so that she knows
she has a voice and she should use it,
she's Chandraghanta.

Raise her to believe
that she's a creator herself
as she is bestowed with a golden womb,
she's Kushmanda.

Raise her to recognize that
she has the power to nurture
and give unconditional maternal love
to any child she bears or raises,
she's Skandamata.
Raise her to understand that
her own two hands

are like having ten and that
not only can she protect herself
but she is capable of being a protector,
she's Katyayani.

Raise her to be a warrior
who fights injustice and intolerance
for she's Kaalratri.
Raise her to know that
she is strong and can bounce
from any ordeal with resilience and grit,
she's Mahagauri.

Raise her to understand that
she isn't half of a whole
but an equal in any partnership,
she's Siddhidatri.

Raise her to never forget that she's Durga,
a culmination of all her nine glorious forms-
Every woman is a goddess!
Every girl deserves to be raised like one-
A goddess of spirit, power and strength.

FREE LOADERS

Focus: fears

How they rise and lurk when I'm not looking,
Sitting astride upon my shoulders, tormenting.
Grubby fingers, tossing about the contents of my brain,
Sipping the last vestige of my energy, they drain.
Powerful agents that abrase, etch and weather,
Leaving me gasping at the very end of my tether_

Oh! How I wish they leave me
and simply disappear
or I find a way
to evict these rent-free tenants, my fears.
They've clutched every facet of my being,

Non-existent scenarios, are all that I'm seeing.
I'm a mere shadow of what I used to be,
Its high time I am all there, just ME.

INHERITANCE

Focus: worries

I'm not afraid, of you turning into me anymore,
the ghosts of our minds *howl* within their trapped confines,
like the wind, they wail,
when they invade the dwellings, of timorous beings.
Ghosts haunt you if you are unable
to read into their deceptively eerie plot lines.
Not many ghouls can puncture the surface,
if you can build a strong demeanour.
Draw hard contracts with devils,
Their disruptions should allow you to claim, force majeure.
Don't become your own prisoner
serving life, in a cloistered hell cell;
Don't ever befriend brutes or let them linger
if you want to be assuaged from assault.
Be unmoved by the haunting roar of ruffians,
bring them to their knees till their whines become whimpers.
They cannot loiter if you have a guarded mind,
they creep in when ingresses are left vulnerable.
None of our ancestors have ever inherited ghosts as a legacy.
So, I won't leave behind, for you, a residue of misgivings
that taints you in the shades of my bruises.
My mind is not a stencil with which you will be outlined,
I'm not afraid of you turning into me anymore;
but you will have your own ghosts to slay, and slay you will
for the will to fight will be your most valued inheritance.

BAKE HAPPY

Focus: outlook

To bake happiness skilfully
measurements are the key.
You need to use top-of-the-rack supplies,
and the temperature needs to be set
to the right degree,

Dreams that have run past their shelf-life
need to be cleared off periodically,
Expectations that were unreasonable
should be sifted out occasionally,
Attachments need to be coated
with a grease-proof baking sheet.

Don't let the crumbs of words and memories
stick or burn into black debris;
Remember it's all about the timing
or your happiness will not rise.
The baking powder that you use
should read "sensible and wise,"

The sunny sunshine butter of hope, should be
at room temperature or else it will not combine,
The sugar that lends the sweetness
should be your peace of mind,

Most importantly the crucial ingredient, is love,
so go all out and use liberally,
Spread it out in a big luscious coat
on strangers, friends and family.
The key ingredient is gratitude,
I'm sharing with you my secret sauce_
And I promise, it will coat every aspect of your life
with a silky shiny gloss.

CAUTION: CONTENTS UNDER PRESSURE

Focus: stress

We should be born with yellow caution tape
wrapped around our (head)
For it is a crime scene,
Where, some of the most sinister thoughts are bred.
Sirens should go off
when we start to berate ourselves.
People around us should be cautioned;
to give them time to brace themselves.
There needs to be a surveillance to check
for every negative thought that craftily entered.
Gate passes should be handed out
to ensure that self-doubts are duly filtered.
Motion cameras should pick up signs
of distress and dejection.
Barricades should be installed
to compartmentalize concerns as per sections.
An intrinsic security service existed within us;
we were supposed to be sheltered by love,
But each of us started to crumble and break
when our responsibilities we began to shove.
If you can find just two arms
(Or four paws)
that can envelope you in an embrace,
You will bounce back from the doldrums
in no time with God's grace.

SECOND SIGHT–SECRET GARDEN

To summarise, Shakti's invisible tape is helping her stay together in spite of adversities while Dev now takes piano lessons, his teacher is empathetic towards his special needs and is incredibly patient with him. Keren is working with her therapist, toward putting the violent episode behind her and Dhairya is learning coping mechanisms to deal with his panic attacks. Gamila has learnt to wear her scars well with the guidance of her counsellor and Atulya is confident and secure that with the unflinching support of his parents the bullies' voices are forever muffled.

Poems stem from triggers, muses, experiences and although these children, men and women around me are real, their names have been changed (in the second sight section of this book) to respect their privacy. Their victory is very real, their proactive steps, taken each day, to work upon themselves are real. Their undaunted families are real and the good fortune of finding competent professionals is real. All of these factors have set my young heroes on a path of growth and positivity.

As a mother, teacher and a keen observer of society around me, what I have learnt through experience is that children possess the art of being opaque and transparent at the same time. They tend to keep their wounds and scars a secret and hence the secret garden of this book is an ode to the innocent minds that harbour these deep-rooted issues. Every generation feels that the next generation has got it all easy but honestly the battles are the same only the weapons change and so do the injuries.

HIDDEN GARDEN

20-65 Age group

THERAPIST THINKS

Mrs. Preeti Kale Kashikar

Pune, Counsellor, internationally certified NLP Practitioner

The age group of 20-65 is a place of conflict for many. This age group needs to deal with a whole gamut of mental health issues that can be triggered by traumatic events of the past, conflicted relationships, changes due to health-related factors, job insecurities, post-partum depression, substance abuse, financial troubles, anger management issues, etc. Recently we have seen a large number of cases between 25- 35 years of age, primarily working women, who are dealing with personality clashes and asserting their identity. Pressures due to social media conditioning give rise to unrealistic expectations and when these are not met it fosters negativity and dejection. Anxiety and the fear of the unknown are the top factors that cause issues. Our intensely competitive world pushes people over the edge in trying to match something unattainable or peer pressure and unreasonable performance expectations from self and others escalate the magnitude of the problems. The pandemic opened the avenues for online sessions and consultations, thereby making it possible to avail therapy or treatment from places that were earlier not practically accessible. Discussions, dialogues, quizzes and several tools are used to assess and advise patients accordingly. Methods like neuro-linguistic programming targets the subconscious mind in order to allow repressed issues to surface so as to plan treatment strategies.

JUGGLER

Focus: Juggling responsibilities

Five,

chubby, grubby fingers,

tugging at the hem of my dress.

I'll sing and play with you, in a bit darling,

Right after I'm done clearing all this mess.

Four,

grubby little fingers,

Incessantly patting on my back,

I'll listen to you! What are you bursting to say?

But my eyes shut the minute I hit the sack!

Three,

grubby not so little fingers,

thrust right into my frustrated face.

Show me how to make shadow deer upon the wall,

Not now, my dear, I'm working on an important case.

Two,

impatient fingers wriggle,

asking for *two* minutes of my time,

Hey! Hold your horses, I'm taking an important call,

stop interrupting, without reason or rhyme.

One,

assertive index finger,

stops me dead in my tracks.

Tables have turned, I'm the one wanting to speak

but doors are slammed, and phones impossible to hack.
Five,
strong decisive fingers,
firmly set to bid an impatient adieu.
I kept being chocked by chores and to-do lists,
While my fledglings left the nest and flew.
All the boxes never got ticked
but time had slipped right through my fingers,
I wish I could turn back time,
I wish I could hold those hands a bit longer.
All I do now is walk down memory lane,
look around my empty house, empty hours and hands.
Wander wistfully amongst faded memories,
as the weight of time, bears down and simply stands.

MIND THE GAP

Focus: depression

I ride the subway every day
dreading its hopeless predictability,
knowing, that the time and price it extracts
is beyond the realms of my affordability.
The doors open and I choose to board_
"Steer clear," a steely voice coldly warns.
Most traps we enter, are at free will;

we still choose to take the bull by its horns.
The train pulls away and picks up speed,
I look up at the neatly printed display.
Each station is clearly marked on the map,
my stomach rolls as I reluctantly ride along the way.
The windows frame, the same old views,
my inertia is sucked into the train's velocity.
As it starts pulling out of duty,
"Next station," the automated voice, declares is ***Reality!***

She has an impersonal faceless voice,
"Doors will open on the right," she says.
The tracking red dot slips into the next spot,
splitting people lengthwise, two ways.

Responsibility, courage, perseverance, hope,
are the next stations that consequently pass.
Commuters approach the inevitable
thrown in unwittingly together en-mass;
Each day I try to carefully chart my route,
come nightfall it's just one thing is realise
my connection to **happiness** keeps giving a slip,
so, plans of **contentment** dwindle and never materialise.

Each day I return, defeated and beaten,
dreading the stations on my return ride.
Stations infamous for their darker side;
knowing that turning around has no upside.

Heartbreak, Despondency, Failure, and Rejection
come one after the other, if not sequentially.
Just bracing to alight at my inevitable destination
has already drained me out fully…
I end up getting off at **depression**
I'm waiting by the door since **indifference.**
This story is repeated over and over again,
In the hope that one day I will find **deliverance.**

BREATHE IN

Focus: existential crisis

Forget everything that
has the ability to scar you for life.
Forget everything
that can transform an ordinary day into hell.
Forget the unfortunate moments
that changed rational to erratic.
Forget that flimsy chance
that slipped through your fingers like quicksand.
Forget the cracking of your heart
when your beliefs were thrashed on the floor.
Forget every emotional attachment and tie
that did not bind you in love and compassion.
Forget everyone around you
that speaks and all you hear is plain noise.
Forget all the time, space and existence
that convinces you to give up on yourself.
Move inward to that space you crafted,
years ago, your very own safe haven.
Envelope yourself in its confines
that paradoxically liberate you.
Then introspect and meditate and wait
till all the frequencies around you go still.
Do this each time you breathe
or you become aware of life within you.
You are yours before anybody else's
and until you rise in your own eyes
there's no real tomorrow.

ARE YOU BEING SERVED?

Focus: loneliness

So many evenings I've sat down with a tall glass of absence.
Sounds uncanny like, Absinthe,
Feels terribly like it, black liquorice -
Leaves a dry burn in the mouth. Familiar?
Three cubes of melancholy, bring in a chill
as a trail of condensation congregates,
enveloping the glass in a grey gloom.
I sit gazing at the evening sky, it speaks,
Animatedly like a linguist; in several languages.
I try translating its wordless monologue,
It's a sad sort of story about endings.
My glass gets colder, heart emptier,
How I wish you could come to sit by me!
There's a chair that I always set out for you
and a glass, and some hope to nibble on.
If you were here the sky would fold upon itself like a blind,
And we would have a night-full of stars,
We wouldn't have our young yesterdays
but all that wouldn't matter because -
My tall glass of absence would be filled,
Right up to the brim, bubbling with your presence.

GHOSTS

Focus: illusions

The ghosts that I've been carrying
were shadows all along.
For decades this weightless burden
tormented me like a haunting song,
all I needed was some clarity,
that came in with the light of the day.
Voids, were all that remained behind
as the shadows slithered away.
Precious time lost for some random voids?
Do our lives amount to this?
We can never find all the pieces,
somethings are bound to remain amiss.
So let voids appear in the day,
let the night bring eerie shadows,
my mind will no longer live in fear;
my resolution is real not a pretence or bravado.

SILENT SCREAMS

Focus: domestic violence

Faded bruises are signs, of what one can inure,
limps and bumps speak, about what one can endure,
blank eyes and taut lips, talk about suffocation and strife-
Trembling fingers and muffled voices
are a testimony of a toxic tangle called life.

They walk amongst us wearing the brightest of smiles,
desperate to hide all the underlying torture and lies.
Sit down with them, firmly hold their hand;
Be there, empathize and understand.
It's easy to judge, to pass a decree,
not everyone has the courage to set themselves free.

Be their rock, their aide, their sounding board.
Help them get safely to liberty road!
And once they do, just see how they bloom
having left behind, the disdain and the doom.
Signs of trouble are usually screams full of silence,
for they mirror a deep-rooted terrifying violence.

TAKE A STAND

Focus: lack of confidence

I'm done with the elephant in the room,
and treading with utmost caution!
I'm done with being politically correct,
weighing words and speaking with dispassion.
I'm done sweeping things under the carpet;
I'm done with non-confrontation!
I'm done walking quietly on tippy toes;
I'm full of impatience and frustration!
Just so that *you* do not rake up trouble,
Just so that no one raises an objection,
While I keep mum and go about my business as usual,
Is there no need for you to take a pause for reflection?
This ends right now and right about here!
You, allow your own subjugation.
I'm officially done with "it's ok,"
And "it has always been like this!"
All these are hopeless instances of vilification!
No, I refuse to be treated with derision,
it's about time I stood up in opposition.
All this while, I've tolerated and it's going on
in the hope that someday there'll be introspection.
Unmute, speak up or leave the table,
Don't sit around moping in vain,
No one said the game of life was easy,
Muster the courage to take a stand for yourself
because at some point you have to learn to rightfully assign
blame!

SEARCH

Focus: asserting identity

To find yourself, you ultimately realize, that you have to lose a crowd.

ODE TO MY KNEES

Focus: chronic physical pain

Out of your massive family of two zero six,
Knee you were the chosen one, like me.
Fate painted the bull's eye on you,
Battered, dislocated, tossed about
Burdened, worn-out, wiped out
with the burgeoning weight of others.
You've always been the sickly one,
Jostled out of sockets, bumped out of luck
With the faintest push, you easily came undone.
Your strength and resolve were tested beyond measure,
And as you weakened the harder you tried,
In your darkest days and inopportune moments,
You may be unaware, but with you, I have cried.
I know the damages are deep and irreversible,
And the trauma is here to stay,
But I'm here to match step for step
Even if together, we walk into the sunset
in a wobbly wabbly kind of way!

HAPPINESS

Focus: unhappiness

Happiness greets, like the setting sun
Late, accompanied by long shadows.

HERD THOUGHTS

Focus: nagging thoughts

I think, I need a herding dog, with my thoughts running astray,
To round them up and send them, trotting down the right way.
They keep wandering in all directions,
lazily grazing on green pastures,
Blissfully unaware, of the fact that they put themselves in danger.
No, there are no wolves lurking,
that would devour my little thoughts,
Fear is, they would get left behind, like a sorry, neglected lot.
A herding dog would drive them,
keep them packed in a tight cluster,
Making sure the formation has no gaps,
he would make their journey safer!
He would ensure that they kept moving,
for lingering behind comes at a cost.
If they have any desire to survive,
they cannot afford to go adrift or get lost.
The guardian dogs, will have just one job,
to make sure each thought stays alive,
For I know all my thoughts have so much to offer
if they get the chance to survive.

CITY SOOTS ME

Focus: struggles of city life

I make do with painted moons on tattered curtains
that distance me from grim views of the city.
It's my mother's saree that the curtains are cut out from,
they still have a lingering smell, of warm meals and hard work,
every whiff of the wind takes me, to a place I once called home.

I close my eyes in weariness, till the window panes shine at dawn.
There is no room for the sun to rise, it needs to find surfaces
to reflect off of and bring in another frenzied day.
There's a faint gap in the curtains
that brings in sunlight very briefly,
till the sun is obscured by the monstrosity
of dwellings that sprout about, like new shoots every day.
My little room with the one window is lit
when a passing train gushes by,
flooding and shaking my abode with light, and sound, and smell
till it plunges back into its dark existence
like a theatre waiting for an act to start.

My eyes are now accustomed to the dark,
the bright lights of the city are too far and too high,
Way beyond my reach or imagination.
It's the blackness within and around that sears and chars,

I'm an extension of the smog and dust
of the exhausts and the vents.
Another discarded entity of the city, I'm now covered
in all the black hues this metropolis exudes and expels!
Each day I feed a piece of me to it, each night **I'm** what the city
regurgitates.

SECRET GARDEN

Focus: unmet expectations

You can keep digging at the same spot
going deeper and deeper,
but you still won't find what you're after.
You will pile up a heap of dirt
which will encircle your ankles
pinning you to the spot and
the hankering to dig a tad bit more
will soon become an obsession.

Move, at the right time,
move on to the right thing,
keep moving till you reach a place
which does not expect you to dig
to find out what lies in store for you;

Look around, the scene may not be picturesque
it might just be too plain and drab
to have caught your eye in the first place,
But one look at it and you can practically read
the words *home* etched upon it
in the most nondescript manner.
It's a place that does not want to impress
or be impressed, it simply allows you to be you.
A milieu that lets you shrug your defences

and lie down with your head pillowed
snugly in the crook of your arm,
No more digging, why seek more when more doesn't exist,
why struggle to grab when nothing is being offered.
It's interesting how a little complacency
at times tells us where to draw lines,
define limits, set boundaries.

All this, so that you stop the grovelling
and rejoice in what lies above the surface
in plain and clear sight,
Your days of digging and abandoning empty holes are over
but the holes won't be wasted,
plant saplings of learnt lessons in them
and watch them bloom.

Lie down and look up at the sky and smile,
for all around you is a garden that takes root in your pain
and emanates the fragrance of your spirit, that survived.

MOON PIES

Focus: parenting struggles

There is something about faint milky breaths,
tiny fingers poking out swaddle sheets;
Something about bright slices of morning sunshine
that become frosty merengue moon pies at night.
About eye locks and plastered downy hair,
about a discarded lone mitten flung across a chair.
About bottles marked with ounces
and tummies that track time,
about worry and joy and exhaustion and elation-
An upbeat roller coaster now
and then, being stuck on a walkalator with frustration.
There's a way about how babies sneak into your hearts,
about how they leave imprints there
and remain tenants even after they leave.
They come tucked in a blankie, dropped off by the stork,
but when they fly the nest
it feels like your heart is struck with a pitchfork.

PURSUIT OF PERFECTION

Focus: unreasonable expectations

Have you seen trees
branching out at ninety degrees?
Or clouds in perfect circles
crafted out of a crispy cold breeze?
Have you seen a dead straight beach,
unyielding to the seas coaxing reach?
Or a moon that refuses to wax and wane,
snatching, the starlit skies, rights in a breach?
The trees bend their backs, hankering for light
while clouds are happier being chubbier than being right.
The beach and sea intertwine their fingers in a wave,
The moon and the stars share the spotlight and behave,
Perfection is a prison, a solitary confinement cell,
An unattainable pursuit, a sinister alarm bell,
Go with the flow,
be fallible,
be free,
Be imperfect, be human, of the finest degree.

LIFELINES

Focus: substance abuse, financial pressures

Sitting cross-legged on an undulated mud floor,
Sun-baked, brown hair, flopping limp on his freckled face_
His eyes moved to his father's hand by the door.
Passed out, he lay sprawled awkwardly, without grace_
"Tell me, Amma, where are Baba's lifelines?"

Smoke scorched her eyes, she swatted stray flies
on her haunches beside the chulha, she cooked,
steam from the boiling rice rose up; wandering
within windowless tin walls that the wind shook,
"What do we do Ma, Baba has no life-lines!"

"I've seen the astrologer under the tree,
he reads out people's fortunes, written within their lines."
She went on with the chores, nursing the baby in hand,
tossing perfectly round rotis with the other.
Life now fails to surprise this impassive woman,
"Tell me, Amma, where are Baba's lifelines?"

"He turned to take yet another closer look,
she still made no attempt to bother.
Baba's stillness could have been exhaustion,
intoxication, one reason or the other,
"What do we do Ma, Baba has no lifelines!"
The little boy peered intently into his father's palm_

A pair of working-class hands, bristly and coarse,
"No wealth line, no health line, so what do we do
with remnants of lines erased out with brute force"?
"Tell me Ma, Baba has no lifelines!"

"Ahh, I get it Amma, now it's crystal clear,
the pesky nagging doubts I've had for so long
are beginning to ebb and reasons seem to appear
so as to why our miseries stay and worries prolong,
"It is because Ma, Baba has no life-lines!"

"I'm the son of a mason who lays hundreds of bricks a day,
but not one of the thousand rooms he builds,
promises a roof upon our head.
He lays long shiny, perfectly moulded kitchen counters bright,
Ready to cook picture-perfect meals, culinary delights,
We cook on a black burnt-out stove,
that smokes more than it steams!

His posh spaces continually realize countless hopes and dreams,
His humble hands are worn and spent in toiling and fulfilling
while our lives dwindle in this sorry excuse of a dwelling.
The more he builds the more we break,
chewed away are our outlines,
Tell me Ma, what lies in my lifelines"?
Looking over her shoulder she said, in a sonorous voice,
"Beta don't sip aspiration from fictitious chalices,
people like us are not born with fortuitous lifelines,
our futures are replaced by embossed calluses!"

ATTITUDE

Focus: attitude

If pain is my reality, endurance is my teacher
if falling is my destiny, rising is my nature,
if life turns out to be a pattern,
living should fill in colour.
The truth is that the right attitude
Can make stepping stones out of failure.

UNSAID

Focus: relationship conflicts

All my unsaid wasted words
fall back into my ribcage;
Auburn words, like autumn leaves,
withered words, whisper and sigh,
slowly twirl, sashay and swoon
sway to psithurism's tunes.
On a day when I can take no more
I sweep them up in pyramidal piles,
smoke emanating
from lit bonfires of my unsaid words,
scalds, my smarting eyes.

PLOY

Focus: verbal attacks

Mellifluous curses served
with rich, honeyed-laced lies,
False façade cannot conceal
shuttered, dishonest eyes.
They come bearing trouble
exuding the nastiest vibes,
The only way to remain unscathed
is to toughen your vulnerable hide.

WEIGHT OF CROWNS

Focus: reality check

There are princesses everywhere,
I see them all around,
Right through the mundane chaos

They are easily seen and found.
Cinderella still keeps darting,
Battling a hostile home situation_
Convinced that to have peace in life,
Running away is her only solution.

Sleeping beauty, is in denial,
Sees no wrongdoing or grave harm,
The gaslighting she faces everyday
is forgotten easily, when he turns on his charm.

Beauty, is pretty delusional.
She believes she can change the beast,
She doesn't realise they are never changing,
Or even attempting in the least.

Snow White, seems to think in numbers,
No, they are all just the same.
They may differ in appearances or demeanour,
But it's the same wine, bottled in a different name.

Rapunzel is kept trapped,
In a prison called the ivory tower,
Convinced that it's for her own good,
She's repressed and clueless of her power.

Princesses need to get a reality check,
Question, oppose and stand up for things you never would,
If you live a life of subjugation,
Your inner fire will be vanquished like wet wood.

LADIES ONLY

Focus: parallel lives

She patted down the pretty pleats
of her fresh fuscia saree.
Coaxing, hurrying her heavy feet_
this last day was not the one to tarry.

For the umpteenth time, she walked
a path that she knew blindfolded;
As flooded memories of centuries
could no longer be withheld.

They had lived a part of their lives
together in a parallel universe,
and everything they did went beyond
exchanging pleasantries and converse!

Vidya could not hide her bruises.
Unabashedly, Sarita wore her bald head.
Rupa sold her nifty, knitted sweaters.
And the day that Kalyani slipped…
she could have ended up dead.

But they all were strongly held on to,
they all had found a faithful friend,
they could all pour their hearts to strangers
who would stand by them and defend.

Netra's pregnant feet were eased with a seat,
Dolly dozed off but missed no scoop,
Bhajiwalis verbally bashed their errant husbands.
Even the coy Malavika, was kept tightly in the loop.

From north to south and south to north,
the local train ran without a hitch;
They got on and off and in and out,
catching their 7:53's without a glitch.

They rushed to and fro, there were clocks to beat,
like cells inside a blood-stream,
rushing duty-bound to make ends meet,
there was very little time to day-dream.

In its confines, a third of their life had gone by;
Life revolved around its whirling wheels,
this lifeline that oxygenated Mumbai
could never be derailed or come to heel.

She broke out of her chain of thoughts,
as she stepped on platform No: 2,
Her last 7:53 pulled into the station
with an uncanny precision as trains do.

She entered the third bogie from the engine
Second class, ladies-only compartment,
Today was her last ride after four decades,
they were celebrating her retirement.

She entered to smiling familiar faces,
some newbies had joined in too
to be adopted into this train family
with warmth that daily commuters do.

They met as strangers on a train,
but ended up exchanging a big part of their lives.
They were organized like busy bees,
What is a commuter train, if not an efficient beehive?

She would miss this crazy buzz,
this vibe, this frantic frenzy,
she knew no other life, than to chug.
The rhythm of her life was tuned
to the rocking of the bogie.

PACIFIER

Focus: vindication

Can vindication heal a piercing wound?
Or does it feel placebo like,
kissing a bruise to make one feel better?
Is a belated vindication better
than never ever getting a reprieve?
Simply accept the crumbs on the table
and say that the meal was delicious?
Can vindication be condescension in disguise?
Appearing to placate but they still get the last word?
Is vindication given in a ditch attempt, at self-correction?
Absolving oneself from the burdens of wrongdoing?
Yet seemingly, they appear the bigger person?
Is vindication necessary even, if you know your truth?
Why does what another person says or does
heal or hurt us?
Are we being enablers of the consequences?
And as much as we cannot control others,
over time, we get addicted to licking our wounds_
It's like a pacifier that keeps us occupied,
it's time to say goodbye to the pacifier,
Liberation is closer, vindication, afar!

WILL WELL

Focus: will power

How do you draw will, from a well that's dry?
How will you know, if you give up and don't try?
There may have been several, seasons of drought,
That you've struggled through and valiantly fought,
There will be showers of respite, if you wait a little longer,
Keep your wits about you, make your determination stronger,
There might be a storm, that brings in a deluge,
You will find several hearts opening, to grant you a refuge,
Wait till the thunder tapers
and the lightning stops tearing the sky,
Wait till the storm water runs off
and the soil gives off a fragrant sigh,
If the earth replenishes her reserves,
you can replenish your resolve,
Watch your doubts douse away, as your fears dissolve,
Your well will be brimming with a new found will,
Draw all you need and you'll have plenty left still.

CALLING

Focus: failure

(Harsh Limericks this girl writes about herself)
There was a girl called Trip,
who was constantly falling,
her clumsy manner was just so appalling.
She went down head first,
completely unrehearsed,
in spite of the fact that
it was her one true calling.

SECOND SIGHT-HIDDEN GARDEN

When I last checked, Pramila had learnt techniques to prioritize her tasks, Arpit had realised that acceptance is the first step taken towards dealing with his issues. Bhushan knew that his turbulent childhood will be his companion always but he's learning how not to be intimidated by it with the help of his counsellor. Sakhi is still not ready to become a volunteer at the NGO to counter her loneliness but she is getting more and more comfortable with her single status, thanks to her monthly sessions with her therapist. Ekta is out of reach of her abusive husband's influence and lives with people who are her support system and whom she trusts. She has learnt that asking for help is not a sign of weakness but the ability to be able to change your circumstances is a sign of strength. Farah has firmly established boundaries in her home with professionals to guide her financially, mentally and legally; she no longer fears for her own life or her son's future. The entire neighbourhood got a glimpse of what a woman can do when Rosa stood up and filed a police case against a local goon who was mentally torturing and threatening her. Her psychiatrist has got her in touch with NGOs that deal with cases like hers. She no longer feels that life is not worth living and is working on her herself with baby steps.

From the eighteen-year-old Farah to fifty-five-year-old Bhushan, what they all had in common was the need to hide their struggles. My hidden garden is where they have buried their trauma and all of them have understood the three milestones on the road to recovery; identify and recognise the issue, discuss and seek professional help and equip yourself with a growth plan. But of course, those that walk the mile are out of the hidden garden onto the highway called 'fulfilling life.'

FORBIDDEN GARDEN

65+ Age group

THERAPIST THINKS

Dr. Jyoti Shetty

MD, DPM Consultant Psychiatrist, Pune

The demography of the Indian population has changed. We have an increasing number of people falling into the "senior citizen" category. This significant "ageing" population suffers from psychological and emotional problems which are largely unmet. They also need to be assessed along with other physical illnesses in order to give their issues an appropriate focus.

Geriatric psychiatry deals with neuro-psychiatric presentations in old age. This age group is different from young people because of the existence of prevailing medical illness & medications, the onset of cognitive impairment and changing psychosocial environment and hence needs to be studied as a separate age group. Stressors are increased, with major life-changing events like losing a spouse, and/or peers, retirement, losing and diminishing social contact, access to healthcare, separation from children, etc.

It is interesting to note that very often people are dismissed as "getting old" but formally old age is classified as, 65-74 young-old, 75 -84 old-old and 85 plus is the oldest- old. A lot of times the obvious changes that are seen are slowing down, orthopaedic issues, inability to multitask with earlier capacity and short-term memory loss along with a host of other issues related to normal body functions. Increased dependency and reduced financial capacity affect them deeply. Elderly people are often burdened with doubts about having fulfilled their responsibilities well towards family and society at large. There is a risk of depression with thoughts of death/self-harm, substance abuse, sleep disorders and anxiety in this age group. Red flags could be a sudden change in behaviour, reduced sleep, incontinence, forgetfulness and fearfulness. Care-givers play a key role for this age group and they need to be reliable and familiar to the needs of patients. With good care-giver education and supervision, improvement in quality of life and psycho-social functioning for patients and families is possible. Care-givers and families need supportive counselling to help cope with financial, physical and emotional strain. In cases like dementia, treatments normally involve caregiver guidance with respect to psycho-education, joining support groups, advise on nursing care, enrolling in memory clinics and handling legal issues apart from medication management. Clinical presentations like delirium need detailed assessment and intervention. Education, awareness, early identification and intervention can help in addressing some of these issues effectively.

HOPE

Focus: dementia

I seem to have forgotten myself,
Don't remind me, of who I once was
For I may never really know him again,
I'll just feel like a lost cause.
Don't remind me of my successes,
Or the trials I've been through,
Don't make me search for missing pieces
That got erased without a clue,
Just stay a little while with me,
Just hear me out as I ramble,
I know I don't make much sense now,
My mind is a hopeless scramble.
I'm struggling and I feel trapped
I'm in this room without a door
The walls are closing in on me
I'm being sucked inside the floor.
The past has been wiped out,
I was robbed of my memories,
The present seems quite strange
I'm full of doubts and worries.
Just throw a lifeline out to me
I'll hold on tightly to the rope,
Remember *you* are all *I've* got,
You hold my future; you are my last hope.

IN MEMORIAM

Focus: bereavement

I kept looking for answers
to all the questions that did not exist,
kept quizzing my mind to find clues
that were misplaced or I had missed.
I wondered what went hopelessly wrong?
Why did your life come crashing to an end?
Like page numbers in a book restrain,
and don't allow chapters to extend.
It is common knowledge, that truth is found
when you read between the lines,
Just then a faded, flattened, faintly fragrant rose,
slipped and fell from its confines.
It had bled colour, where it was rooted to a spot,
like a prisoner of a past that wastes away and pines.
When I think of you, I open this book,
time and memories are in fact cages,
our lives together will lie here for eternity.
Forever stuck between the pages.

DISENGAGE

Focus: separation anxiety

With every choice you make,
the umbilical cord is cut yet again.
Putting spaces between us-
expanding the paces between us,
until a time comes that you are so distant
my outstretched hands become the diameter.
Spanning an empty sanctuary
that you have now exited.

Outside, you are in a wilderness,
a land alien to me.
I do not understand its landscape
and I have no knowledge of the predators.
Yet I'm more afraid of what you will do to yourself
than what that world will do to you.

With every step you take
the umbilical cord turns and twists
as if to hold you back.
It struggles to reach out and hold you down;
in a frenzied desperation to keep you safe.

The truth is that the cord has been severed.
It may struggle, resist and try and hold you back
but it will always lose.
It's *'your'* journey
and it will be charted by *'your'* choices
and in them are my prayers.
when you make each of those choices
place your hand over your gut.

It will always tug, nudging you
in a direction that allows you to make
the right choice, a prudent choice!
A healthy choice, a positive choice
and especially the kind of choice
that helps you keep your head held up high,
and your heart filled with contentment.

FALLEN LEAVES

Focus: isolation

Fallen leaves
cling on to their trees,
Making their way back
into its hollow,
Lying in pleading heaps,
They softly weep,
Rustling in a litter
of their own sorrow.
Damp tears, tear them
tethered apart...
Distraught, they breathe their last
on forest floors,
Crumbling into the soil their souls,
Give form to new lives rising
from their cores!

CHOICES

Focus: questioning choices

The train to **Regret** always arrives late!
Passengers waiting to get to **Closure**
perpetually miss their connection,
Anger, the nonstop superfast express
comes to a grinding halt only at **Destruction.**
Too Late, the abandoned station on that line
is where most people are stranded inordinately!
Over Thinking, tends to dangerously derail.
Embarking, on it, is completely at one's own risk.
Trust, is a two-way train, no questions asked.
Return tickets need to be bought upfront.
Anticipation, is a troublesome all-nighter.
No guarantees of sleeping on that one.
Sadness, is a slow train, moves at a snail's pace;
overcrowded but paradoxically a lonely ride,
And then there's **Surprise**, it arrives out of **Nowhere.**
No destination is ever listed for that one.
But the one that's most popular is **Joy**.
That's one quick trip, finished even before it starts-
The safest one to book yourself on though,
Is **Acceptance**, no matter what you get "there"
You navigate **Life** on multiple trains,
when you decided **when** and **where** to go
and your destiny is shaped with the
How, which is what you end up paying as fare.

ISLANDS

Focus: neglect

People are like islands,
Separated by the deepest seas,
Seemingly put so close together,
But hardly visible or seen.
Every island holds a volcano in its gut,
that keeps threatening to burst,
Sadly the waters that enclose it,
Just cannot quench its thirst,
Every island has sandy beaches,
Lined with pretty sparkling shells,
that the storms keep ravaging,
and seem to have no intention to quell.
Some islands submerge in oblivion,
They were no one's priority to save,
Sometimes it's shallow waters that drown,
Does not always take a tidal wave!

UNFINISHED

Focus: accepting uncertainty

It is better to have unread pages in the story of our life
than unwritten ones,
Skipped pages just tell a different story!
Save the pages where the ink dried out and the tears poured,
Mark the ones where the margins were full
but your heart was empty,
Annotate every synonym that tried to mask the word *pain*,
Underline the sentences that defied grammar rules
yet made sense only to you,
You are always a work in progress, building chapter after chapter,
But the end is neither up to you nor can you write it.
We are *all* but unfinished novels in different stages after all.

STRENGTH

Focus- resilience

Standing tall has little to do with the strength or length of my feet.

MANUPLATIVE VERB

Focus: regret

I think that the one thing I truly regret
in my life, is regretting itself.
Regretting lost friends and friendships,
Regretting lost time and opportunities,
Regretting lost skills and experiences,
Regretting, neglecting oneself.

But I reckon regrets are lessons…
…building blocks to be used to rebuild.
We are born out of a womb,
presumably, pre-labelled and limited
by our defining DNA's,
but our lives are opportunities to crack templates,
to explore and be emotionally pliable,
a chance to bend and break,
cut and trim, stretch and reach.

Submitting to change isn't a sign of weakness,
there is maturity in accepting the inevitable.
If regret can be transmuted into becoming a manipulative verb,
the shape of our life will be resolutely redefined.

QUESTIONS

Focus: hard on self

If *WHY* is the biggest tormentor,
Then *WHAT IF* is a sadist.
If *WHEN* remains unanswered,
then *MAYBE* is a pessimist.
Hurling questions at the mind like darts
hoping to hit the bull's eye,
Will only result in it being repeatedly hurt.
When this self-inflicted torture ends,
life begins, mental peace is possible,
when our thinking is rooted in acceptance
and our reactions embrace change.

WAITING GAME

Focus: terminal illness

I'm waiting,
long sighs,
empty eyes waiting and waiting...
twiddling thumbs, feeling numb,
I'm still waiting...
night turns to days, days corrode away
forever waiting,
time inches by- years seem to fly,
I'm constantly waiting...
there's no escape room,
there's a foreboding sense of doom
as I've been waiting,
the worst is here.
Everyone far and near
is also now waiting...
this waiting room has no door
the air is stagnant and sour
I'm waiting, I'm waiting
Just promise you will be by my side
While I'm waiting…

ARMOUR

Focus: vulnerability

I feel the waves coming right up to my mouth
and receding back to my heart,
There is an overwhelming desire to let out,
this sea of turbulence out into the universe,
But I hold back with every reserve I have,
for you must never see my sorrow
for I have kept it in my possession
like a treasure that no one can ever see.
But who can stop the moon from playing
this cruel game of gravitation?
I'm torn between the highs and lows
while the moon feigns innocence,
But you, must always, see me still and serene,
lost in a meditative calm,
Don't come near the water's edge I pray,
or you will hear my spasmodic sobs of sorrow,
Don't pelt my porcelain pretence,
for it is not my mask but my armour instead.

MISALIGNED

Focus: agitation

The jagged edges of the mind
gnaw, gash and grind.
Thoughts get sliced like paper cuts;
unseen wounds bleed being undermined.
Hurtful memories rust over time,
release them from being confined.
Purge out the junk before it can intertwine,
become enshrined.
Lodged deep in places so hard to find, undefined!
Oblivious are we, of what gets left behind;
troubled minds;
tangled and misaligned.

CENTRE

Focus: being centred

When you become a home to somebody,
your body becomes stone and mortar.
You dig your feet in, twenty feet below the ground,
till your soles are blistered, pressed against hard rock,
Your ankles swell in the water-logged soil,
your shins push back the earth that threatens to cave in.
Your lap cradles generation after generation,
your waist gets accustomed to encircling arms
of those seeking refuge
Your ribs securely safeguard your inhabitants,
your heart mimics the moon and wanes and waxes
opening and closing doors as people enter and exit,
Your bosom nurtures the progeny!
With a steady supply of salubrious subsistence,
your shoulders mutate into mantle pieces,
Displaying artifacts, articulating timelines.
Your neck turns reluctantly,
towards directions dictated by destiny,
Your mouth becomes a repository
retrieving the old, restoring the damaged.
Your eyes await the arrivals and dread the departures,
and your mind becomes a tangle of thoughts, a field of worries,
When you become a home to somebody all paths lead to you.
You become somebody's centre of the universe.
Question is,
is your own centre, centred yet?

PHANTOM LIMBS

Focus: trauma

Some odd trees grow in quicksands,
taking birth in drowning hands;
growing in agitated viscous soil
roots nourished by turmoil.
Rising to unprecedented heights,
uprooted, transplanted, taking flights.
Fighting survival in alien worlds,
struggling barks, twisted, swirled,
roots saturated with memories of strife.
Battling branches grab sunlight.
Time relents, skies turn sunny and blue-
an evergreen canopy basks in full bloom,
yet the tree weeps silent tears and cries,
a niggling wound gnaws at its insides.
Phantom roots still fight the old quicksand,
the tree now stands in a lush grassland
even if the limbs are gone and long forgotten;
The pain is real, scorching and molten.
Douse today, every searing, burning ember,
severed pasts tend to infest the mind forever.

IN JE(U)ST

Focus: apathy

Offensive things take birth in the garb of jest.
Are pampered by unchecked recklessness and silence,
Grow up to be uncaring and hostile.

MORE THAN WAITING

Focus: memory loss

I'm more than someone who's just waiting,
For the inevitable and the impending,
I'm somebody hidden but not in hiding,
I'm somewhere here in case your searching...

I'm locked memories and history,
I'm an elaborate but a worn-out tapestry,
I'm relationships and sacrifices,
I'm unable to distinguish between masks and guises,

I'm part of people that parted and departed,
I'm unable to finish, to remember how it started,
I'm a shadow of my once distinct existence,
I'm full of nothingness that lives with material abundance,

I'm unreachable but still a bit around,
I'm waiting to be seen not misplaced to be found,
I'm blank emotionless eyes and lost smiles,
I'm past false truths and present true lies,

I'm about holding hands and leafing through time,
I've forgotten what's yours once used to be mine,
I'm more than *just* someone that's waiting,
For the inevitable and the impending,
I'm somebody hidden but not in hiding,
I'm trapped in a mind that is fast closing in and confining!

A BRIDGE TO NO WHERE

Focus: lack of purpose

My roads have been washed out,
My river has changed its course,
I'm left standing here, so pointless-
With all my might, my strength, my force.
Now that my roads have been washed out,
Now that my river has changed its course,
I wonder what I was thinking?
When I thought, all I needed, was to reinforce?
Fact is, my roads have been washed out,
Fact is, my river has changed its course.
I've just stood here now for quite some time,
All my loud thinking has turned me hoarse!
I miss my roads that were washed out,
I long for my river that changed its course,
I'm a bridge going nowhere,
My empty banks are full of remorse.
Can I build back the roads that were washed out?
Will my river ever return by changing its course?
Sometimes the answers do not lie within us,
Sometimes they are binding and enforced,
Sometimes bridges going nowhere,
Rely on a hope that is outsourced!

POWER PLAY

Focus: losing peers

Some flew,
Some stayed,
Some bid adieu…
I remain humbled
watching nature's
power play!

OBSESSED

Focus: dissatisfaction

I asked a fisherman casually
"So, what did you catch today?"
With a glint in the eye, he looked at me
in the most unnerving kind of way
he was almost looking into my soul
when he very wisely began to say,
"Aren't you the one that is obsessed
with the things that slip away?"

WHAT YOU DONT KNOW ABOUT ME!

Focus: indifference

You scoffed and laughed as I wiped a tear
when I said goodbye to my car of eighteen years;
There's a lot you don't know about me…

You have no idea how many times
the frantically waving wipers on her windshield
felt helpless as they worked at keeping
the rain off of my vision but could do little
to wipe my tears that blocked my path.
There's a lot you don't know about me…

You say I hoard unnecessary trash,
but in fact, what I do is trap time
like, in that ticket stub from the movie theatre_
I tucked a memory of how your profile looked
in the reflected light of the screen as it fell on your face
and with all the courage I could muster
I had stolen a few sideways glances.
There's a lot you don't know about me…

Like how I talk to my plants and watch
the birds take dips in make-shift bird baths
and I've given them each a special name
because crow sounds rude and robin is too impersonal
and I know how impersonal feels.
There's a lot you don't know about me...

Like how in the nights, I sit down with insomnia
and we play twenty questions and
every day, insomnia beats me hollow
yet I play every night, not because I hope to win
but because there are more than twenty other things
that leave me alone until dawn.
Clearly, there's a lot you don't know about me...

For every time I speak to you
all the unspoken and unsaid get lodged in my throat
so bad that I begin to gag and just about then
you turn your back, yes, the *one* that I speak to most of the time
and you say, for the hundredth exasperating time,
"See, I can read your mind, no one knows you better than me!"

I sigh and whisper,
"There's a lot you don't know about me"!

BLANK WALLS BLEED

Focus: building walls

She was a wall, hardened,
strong, sturdy on the outside
hollow, crushed and crumbling inside.
The layers of paint slapped on her facade,
fooled all but me...

I could see the slight surface cracks,
faint, nondescript almost non-existent,
she cleverly blamed the elements;
Said the summer heat left her flushed
while the winters pinched her joints.

She stood there, stood and stood some more,
a silent spectator of her own life
vacantly gazing out of a window,
Oh! How she longed to be free.

To feel the first drops of the rain on her cheeks,
to feel the cool breeze, linger upon her face,
but she was a wall, rooted, pinned to a spot,
weighed down by wanting, weary of waiting.

The spasmodic arms of an imaginary clock upon her chest
monotonously ticked off minutes,
an indication of passing time,
I looked at her blank visage wistfully,
How can someone be this broken?
yet stand solidly without breaking?

Sometimes, it is not "how" someone is broken
that moves us, more often,
the way they hold up together, tears us apart.
I want to reach out and say I see all your wounds,
the gashes, the gaps, the gorges.
Your brokenness, I may not be able to heal,
but I'm here to bandage, help repair and seal;

Sometimes the injuries are not in plain sight to see,
Walled-up souls tend to internally bleed.

UNKEMPT GARDEN

Focus: healing

Right behind my heart, there is a secret path,
Leading to a grave in a garden unkempt.
A well-worn, weather-beaten flowerless trail,
takes me to this quiet hideout that I frequent.
I've spent many an hour lamenting here.
In the company of silence and isolation.
Sat cross-legged, amidst the overgrowth;
seeking my own forgiveness and reconciliation.
My heart is unforgiving when it comes to me.
My weeping eyes are weary with pain.
But this coldest frozen part of my heart;
shows no signs of relenting or refrain.
All the warmth I have, radiates out of my heart,
Embracing others with love and empathy,
Yet when it comes to being kind to myself,
My heart is brutal and extends only apathy.
I now go back to the grave of my broken soul,
I'm trying to gently rouse it back to life,
Bit by bit I'm going to build it whole,
Self-love will make the brokenness come alive.

SECOND SIGHT–FORBIDDEN GARDEN

It's interesting how Shankar Kaka does not recognise me, but he can instantly differentiate between a Manna Dey song from a Rafi song when I play him his CDs. Music therapy and intervention at the right time have indeed changed his quality of life. Vidya Tai picks the loveliest *Prajakta* flowers to adorn her late husband's photo, it was good that Sharad decided to take her to a therapist after all, she's dealing with the loss a lot better. The Vermas and their three NRI sons have worked out a mutually favourable arrangement so the empty nest feels a little less stark, their therapist has guided on how to train attendants and nursing staff that take care of aunty who is mostly confined to a wheelchair. The uncle on the sixth floor has stopped blaming himself for his alcoholic son and the whole family is seeking professional help to get things back on track. They all know that the obstacles in their path were so huge and formidable that they had raised a towering cocoon around themselves where outsiders were forbidden to step into.

Just a tiny wicket gate helped to end their self-imposed exile and the first thing they did when the path to normalcy started to emerge out of the fog of uncertainty, was to embrace the second chance; hold on to the lifeline thrown at them and let out all the suffocating anguish out of their lives.

It takes just a knock on the door of a professional, a few sessions with a therapist, a couple of years of taking the right guidance from a trained expert or years of tireless, unrelenting, dedicated service as a care-giver, or availing longterm treatment as an ailing patient. You might keep it a secret, you can hide it as cleverly as possible, you may forbid people from puncturing your disguised veneer and choose an arduous lonely ride. Or you can share, seek and open yourself to find answers, solutions and hope.

AFTERWORD

This book is an outcome of my tryst with mental health issues that I've confronted with as an individual, and as a strong, supportive care-giver to family and friends who reached out to me for help or for whom I was responsible. Having suffered a chronic medical condition for more than three decades, physical pain was no stranger to me. Yet, in 2017, I started finding certain changes in my thinking and behaviour that were completely alien to me. Being an extremely practical person and an optimist at heart I was unable to deal with this new "me" that acted and thought completely out of character. I picked up myself and sought the help of Dr. Jyoti Shetty, who diagnosed me with clinical depression and began my treatment which was a combination of medication and therapy. It was not an easy journey for sure, as I was feeling tremendous apprehension, confusion and fear of undergoing this treatment. Yet thanks to Dr. Shetty I soon started looking at mental health issues just like the other health issues I had dealt with on a regular basis, in the past. The therapy and medicines helped me gather myself and surge ahead with renewed gusto. At this point, I began to express myself through poetry and till date have written over 700 poems in the last three years. I started sharing my poems on my Instagram account *"@foundavoice."* Writing poetry was a cathartic and liberating experience for me. I truly believe nothing has the power to heal as much as art does.

Another time I took a mental health issue heads on was my father's brain stoke and dementia he suffered after that. When your parent looks at you with zero recognition in their eyes, it is the most gut-wrenching experience for any child and I was completely devastated when this happened with me. My father, a gifted, brilliant mathematician forgot everything; family, mathematics, even who he was! It was the unrelenting persistence, sacrifice and dedication of my mother and the will of God and modern medicines that we got him back to a functioning degree. He was never his original self but he tried his level best to accept his situation and till his last days, a few years later, he never gave up on himself.

I've been closely involved in a situation where a child was suffering from physical and mental trauma due to illness and environmental issues and I've witnessed how therapy helped identify the reasons for the child's changed behaviour and personality and helped the child to return to normalcy thanks to the efforts of Dr. Shetty and Dr. Mridula Apte.

Parents go through a series of emotions where at first, they are in denial, then they accept the situation with reluctance, following which they become a proactive and complete support system for the child emotionally. Eventually, they learn that neither the child nor the parent is to be fully blamed for the unfortunate situation they find themselves in. Through my friends and acquaintances, issues like domestic violence, infidelity, frustration in career, home issues, failing relationships, lack of finances and parenting problems made me stare at a host of reasons that lead to mental health issues in the society around us. Each man or woman that faced these issues made me more aware of the realities of our society and that mental health issues exist regardless of being economically secure or having a good education. The taboo attached to seeking help for mental health issues has been the reason that so many people and their families unnecessarily suffer endlessly. The purpose of this book is to spark a ray of hope in the minds of the readers and encourage them to seek help to overcome problems.

This book is for anyone that connects with any of the poems that are a part of this collection. If I can encourage you to seek help, break barriers and overcome hurdles then and only then would this book mean anything to me personally. I have outstretched my hand with hope and anticipation that more will come forward to help themselves and others. Together we can make a huge difference in creating a mentally healthy society.

ABOUT THE AUTHOR

Asmita Patwardhan is a poet, architect, mother and academician. She won the jury award, for poetry at the TataLitLive fest in 2019, for her poem titled "Phantom Roots". She won the second prize in a short story competition organised by ISOLA, Mumbai in the year 2020 for her entry titled Gangu's Grove". Her poetry has figured in three anthologies of national and international publications. She has co-authored and published an anthology titled "Three Women in a Boat" along with two other poets.

She has written three research papers on subjects like architecture and heritage, which have been published in national and international journals. She has written several technical articles for Indian publications and has been a content writer for websites related to art and architecture.

Made in the USA
Monee, IL
07 July 2026

56644423R00080